1918-1934
From the Merrill C. Berman Collection

Lutz Becker

Richard Hollis

National Touring Exhibitions
Hayward Gallery
South Bank Centre, London

Published on the occasion of
Avant-Garde Graphics:
1918-1934
A National Touring
Exhibition organised by
the Hayward Gallery, London
for Arts Council England

Exhibition tour:

1 October – 27 November 2004
Hunterian Art Gallery, Glasgow
4 December 2004 –13 February 2005
Glynn Vivian Art Gallery, Swansea

23 March – 5 June 2005
Estorick Collection of Modern Italian Art,
London

Tour continues

Exhibition curated by Lutz Becker
Exhibition organised by Roger Malbert
and Henrike Ingenthron

Catalogue designed by Richard Hollis
with James King
Art Publisher: Caroline Wetherilt
Publishing Co-ordinator: James Dalrymple
Sales Manager: Deborah Power
Printed in England by the Oaktree Press

Published by Hayward Gallery Publishing,
London SE1 8XX, UK
© Hayward Gallery 2004
Texts © the authors 2004
Artworks © the artists / estates of the artists
(unless otherwise stated)
Photographs courtesy the Merrill C. Berman
Collection © Jim Frank, unless
otherwise stated

ISBN 1 85332 238 5

Hayward Gallery Publishing titles are
distributed outside North and South America
by Cornerhouse Publications,
70 Oxford Street, Manchester M1 5NH
T +44 (0)161 200 1503
F +44 (0)161 200 1504
E publications@cornerhouse.org
www.cornerhouse.org/publications

◀ Front cover:
Unemployed, Berlin 1931
Photo: Willy Römer, ABZ Berlin

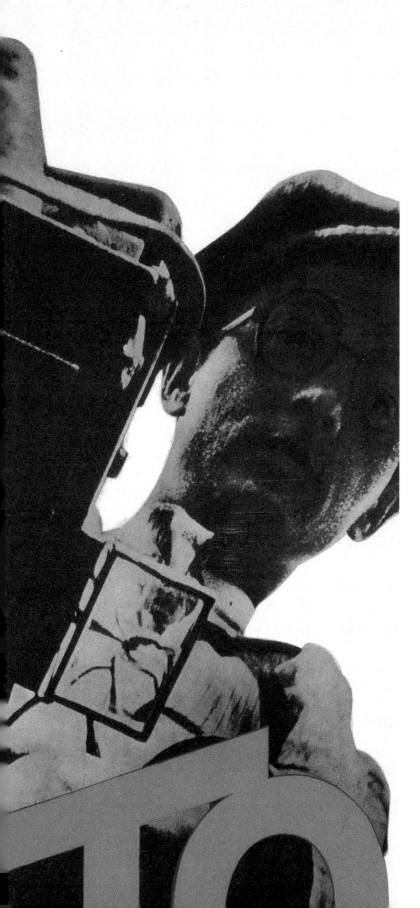

Contents

◀ Designer unknown
**Film and Photo International Exhibition
Stuttgart**
Poster (detail),1929
Cat.4

▶ Overleaf:
Max Burchartz
Red Square
Collage (detail), c.1928
Cat.24

Preface

■ **Avant-Garde Graphics: 1918-1934** brings together 150 rare posters, original designs, collages and photomontages from the Merrill C. Berman Collection, Rye/New York, one of the most important private collections of Modernist art and design in the world. Thanks to the great range and excellent condition of these works – including not only posters of iconic status but artworks and original layouts – this exhibition gives a direct insight into the creative struggles that drove the development of modern visual communication and design in the early twentieth century. In a manner not dissimilar to the graphologist who can reveal individual character traits and psychological dispositions through the study of handwriting, the student of Modern art can discover in the evolution of modern visual design the 'signature' of an age, which reveals the prevailing trends in European societies between the wars.

■ The collector Merrill C. Berman grew up in a Jewish family near Boston, Massachusetts. He studied history and political science at Harvard University during the late 1950s. His knowledge and understanding of the history of art and graphic design led him to collect important works of poster art, book design and political ephemera. His interest as a collector has been focused primarily on the groundbreaking works of the artists and designers of the European avant-garde. Merrill C. Berman's career as a research analyst and investor has enabled him to assemble one of the most comprehensive archives of its kind. His collection documents every stage of Modernist development in the twentieth century and rivals in quality, cohesion and range most public collections in the United States, Europe and Japan. His choice of artists includes most of the famous names in the field, as well as lesser-known figures that he has re-discovered and brought to prominence.

■ The marvellous wealth of Merrill C. Berman's collection was first revealed in Britain in Tate Modern's exhibition *Century City: Art and Culture in the Modern Metropolis* in 2001, to one section of which, on Moscow in the 1920s (curated by Lutz Becker), he lent a substantial number of posters, photomontages and drawings. *Avant-Garde Graphics* allows us to see a greater range of material from his collection, and his generosity in allowing us to tour some of his most outstanding works is warmly appreciated. We thank too Jim Frank for his invaluable help in preparing the exhibition and for kindly providing us with photographs of the works.

■ *Avant-Garde Graphics* was proposed to us as a National Touring Exhibition by the filmmaker, historian ànd curator Lutz Becker, a longstanding friend of the Hayward Gallery. He has been closely involved in the origination of a number of major Hayward exhibitions from *Art and Revolution* in 1971 and *Piscator and Political Theatre* in 1972, to *The Romantic Spirit in German Art 1790-1990* in 1994 and *Art and Power: Europe under the dictators 1930-45* in 1995. Lutz Becker has also advised and encouraged us in many vital ways during the past three decades. We are grateful to him for helping to realise this powerful exhibition, a reminder of the imaginative freedom and formal daring of Modern art and design in the early twentieth century, and thank him too for his highly informative introductory essay in this publication.

■ We thank Richard Hollis, who has designed this catalogue and has also contributed to the book an insightful and authoritative essay on the graphic design of the avant-garde. The catalogue's editing and production needs have been the responsibility of Caroline Wetherilt, the Hayward's Art Publisher, and James Dalrymple, our Publishing Co-ordinator, and I extend particular thanks to them for their expertise and attention to every detail of the book.

■ The exhibition was first discussed and developed under the directorship of Susan Ferleger Brades, and we remain grateful to her for her commitment and support. Helen Luckett, the Hayward's Resources Programmer, has produced an extensive range of interpretative material with her usual care and skill. Imogen Winter, the Hayward's Registrar, has organised and overseen the shipping of the exhibits and their transport within the UK, the latter with Transport Foreman, Dave Bell.

■ It has been a great pleasure to work with our colleagues in the exhibition's host galleries, all of whom have responded with unhesitating enthusiasm to the project from the start: Mungo Campbell at the Hunterian Art Gallery, Glasgow; Karen MacKinnon and Jenni Spencer-Davies at the Glynn Vivian Art Gallery, Swansea; and

Roberta Cremoncini at the Estorick Collection of Modern Italian Art in London. Each of these venues in a different way provides an appropriate context for the exhibition, which we hope will stir the imaginations of a new generation of graphic artists and designers.

■ Finally, my thanks go to Henrike Ingenthron, Assistant Exhibition Organiser at the Hayward Gallery, for her close attention to every aspect of this project and for bringing it to fruition.

Roger Malbert
Senior Curator, Hayward Gallery

▶ Overleaf:
Piet Zwart
Radio Station Scheveningen
Brochure cover, 1929
© DACS 2004
(Not in exhibition)

ONTWERP P. ZWART

Lutz Becker

Dynamic City Design and Montage

■ Industry and War

The machine age reached its peak in the early twentieth century. Industrial production redefined the way humanity divided labour and wealth. The mass distribution of goods from all over the world opened up new horizons and introduced a sense of internationalism. Rapidly advancing science freed hitherto unknown energies. Electricity took over from steam as t he main source of primary power. City lights began to turn night into day and filled the streets with unfamiliar sights. The sensation of speed became commonplace through the invention of the motorcar and the aeroplane. Novel means of communication – the telephone, teleprinter and radio – enabled distant peoples of different nations to share their news and ideas. The spread of photography and film altered the way humanity saw itself.

■ New kinds of possibilities and creative sensibilities evolved. A young generation of artists crossed the threshold to modernity. These artists formed the avant-garde of the new, spearheading the discovery of hitherto unexplored territories of the imagination. The search for contemporary forms of expression reached a forceful presence in architecture and engineering, but also in the experimental beginnings of a new formal language in painting, sculpture and graphic art informed by Cubism and abstraction. An efficient design canon, derived from the vocabulary of mechanical engineering and architectural construction, made a larger public aware of the aesthetics of the machine and geometric forms.

■ 'We praise war, the only hygiene of the world', was one of the most provocative statements contained in the founding manifesto of the Futurists, published on the front page of the Paris newspaper *Le Figaro* in February 1909. The author was the Italian poet and entrepreneur Filippo Tommaso Marinetti. War was seen by him and an affiliated circle of young artists as the healing shock, the only way to end bourgeois stagnation, to free a society imprisoned in its conventions, traditions, rituals and prejudices. This group wanted modernising reforms and political changes and was ready to bring about the end of the old order, if necessary, by force. While Marinetti hoped that the expected cataclysm would be the 'cleansing' blood bath, which would produce the condition for the radical renewal of the world, the Russian revolutionary V.I. Lenin believed that war would result in the Socialist revolution.

■ The ruptures of the First World War and revolutions in Russia and Germany between 1914 and 1918 finally resulted in the breakdown of established political structures, social order and cultural cohesion in Europe. The subjective worldview of the pre-war years was replaced by a more scientific and objective perspective. The unified vision of the Renaissance world, which had so far provided the framework for human aspirations and an assured sense of completeness, even contentment, was shattered; alienation and the unsettling sensation of fragmentation took its place. Thus began an age of uncertainty.

■ Revolution seemed for many a necessary step towards the renewal of society; some countries aimed for the creation of a democratic republic as the only way to regain a sense of completeness, others saw their future in a dictatorship. Many political solutions were on offer; it was hard to differentiate between genuine options and the mirage of Utopia. The great cities became the centres of a newly-found, often radically-pursued freedom. Political parties, mass movements and artistic and literary groups entered the public arena. The streets became their battleground.

Filippo Tommaso Marinetti
Words (Consonants Vowels Numbers) in Freedom / After the Battle of the Marne Joffre inspects the front by car
Journal, 1919
© DACS 2004
(Not in exhibition)

■ City and Design

In his poem *Zang-tumb-tumb*, published in 1914 at the outbreak of the First World War, and his manifesto *Parole in Liberta* (Words in Freedom) of 1913 and 1919, the Futurist Marinetti broke the rules of syntax and unhinged the linearity of texts. He collaged text fragments with freely-associated, onomatopoeic word creations, thus giving full legitimacy to the world of noise and verbal abstraction. Futurists from Italy and Russia and Dadaists from Germany and France followed suit. Under Marinetti's leadership, the Futurists – Umberto Boccioni, Ardengo Soffici, Giacomo Balla and Fortunato Depero – aimed to overcome the limitations of two-dimensionality in painting, sculpture and graphic design by introducing the elements of time, dynamism and simultaneity.

Johannes Baader
and Raoul Hausmann
Dada Milky Way
Poster, 1918
Cat.7

■ In 1916, at the height of the war, the Berlin Dadaists John Heartfield and George Grosz produced their first montages, which contained painting and photographic components, and established the method of photomontage and its terminology. Their montages, published in the magazine *Neue Jugend* (New Youth) and presented in Dada exhibitions, reflected the Dadaist rejection of old social hierarchies and bourgeois values. To renew art the old had to be destroyed. The defunct military class, which was still attached to nineteenth-century values, and academic artists who had served the monarchy before the war were under attack. Anti-establishment activism produced anti-art, provocative poetry and imagery, a fitting response to the cruel absurdities of life in war-time Berlin: sometimes charmingly silly and anarchistic, at other times aggressively controversial, lampooning political enemies.

■ Dadaists adopted, mixed and extended texts and fragments of newsprint with found images and photomontages. Despite the fact that Dada was a short-lived episode in the story of the German avant-garde, the impact of artists like Johannes Baader and Raoul Hausmann, Hannah Höch and Kurt Schwitters was enormous. Playfully, they broke typographic conventions and expanded the print medium by fusing text with photographic images.

■ Futurism and Dadaism were reactions to the prevailing sense of discontinuity, symptoms of a fragmented reality. By the end of the First World War other art movements had emerged in Europe that turned towards the analysis of the post-war condition and tried to define an art relevant to contemporary society. Around the Dutch painter Theo van Doesburg gathered a group of artists including Piet Mondrian, Bart van der Leck and Mart Stam. In 1919, they founded the magazine *De Stijl*, which was dedicated to uniting painting, architecture and design.

■ They were soon joined by the graphic designers Paul Schuitema and Piet Zwart, who emphasised in their work geometric purity and the reduction of design to the most functional essentials. Both Schuitema and Zwart provided graphic designs for industry as well as for the left magazine *Links Richten* (Towards the Left) and were active as members of the Union of Worker Photography. In addition to their typographic innovations, both designers utilised photomontage in their work, creating both persuasive commercial advertising and eloquent political campaigns.

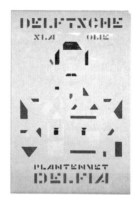

Bart van der Leck
Delft Salad Oil
Design for poster, 1919
Cat.61

■ This was the time when cinema was maturing into a medium of mass entertainment, radio had become available to increasing numbers of households, and the electric amplification of public speeches by politicians and agitators was beginning to influence the masses with overwhelming directness. Simultaneously, the visual language of public imagery – of posters, advertisements and illustrated magazines – went through a period of radical change. The multidisciplinary engagement of many of the Modernist artists and designers carried them into the centre of political and commercial activity; their productions reached the masses. Interconnected with the growing range of other mass media, radio, film and theatre, the increasing influence and power of print media and advertising brought about the emergence of modern mass communication.

■ Throughout the 1920s, Berlin was at the crossroads of European politics; contesting ideologies on the left and the right fought each other with a fervour akin to religious warfare. Individual interests and the collective aspirations of the urban masses became competing poles. Commercial life was marked by high expectations in industrial-scientific progress and mass production. Berlin, an international centre for contemporary art and design, acted as catalyst and collecting-point for new ideas, which underwent an instant testing in this aggressive milieu. Life in the city had an exciting experimental flair: trends, fashions and political positions seemed to change daily. Advertising covered hoardings and poster columns and colourful newspaper kiosks displayed illustrated magazines that disseminated a kaleidoscopic range of images. As social and political realities changed, so did the images, which reflected that reality.

Oskar Schlemmer
The Triadic Ballet
Poster, 1922
Cat. 90

■ The design culture emanating from the Bauhaus (established in 1920 in Weimar, and in Dessau from 1925 onwards), was emblematic of the progressiveness of Weimar Germany. The Bauhaus had developed, under the directorship

of the architect Walter Gropius, into one of the most influential schools of art and design in Germany. Amongst those who taught at the school were the painters Paul Klee, Vasilii Kandinsky, Oskar Schlemmer and László Moholy-Nagy. Their workshops were driven by new teaching methods derived from current art practice, the exploration of materials and design procedures.

Joost Schmidt
**State Bauhaus Exhibition /
Weimar**
Poster, 1923
Cat. 91

■ The didactic innovations of the Bauhaus were taken up by art schools throughout Germany. A comprehensive foundation course led students to experiment with a new creative vocabulary and to exercise risk-taking and design responsibility. Committed to a functionalist ethos, Bauhaus artists and students re-interpreted craft traditions and created prototypes fitting the requirements of industry and mass production. The influence of Moholy-Nagy and Herbert Bayer was to change the face of Bauhaus graphics and photography. In their eyes modern graphic design was the visible synthesis of typographic and photographic information. For the independent designers Kurt Schwitters from Hanover and Jan Tschichold from Munich, the Bauhaus was a centre of gravity with which they had frequent contact. Their work and personal example defined the Bauhaus style, which revolutionised in its boldness, economy, composition, printing and reproduction processes. Bauhaus theory and practice became the foundation of modern visual communication.

■ The Russian artist El Lissitzky was an energetic mediator between east and west. In 1922 he organised the first exhibition of Russian art in Western Europe – *Erste Russische Kunstausstellung* (First Russian Art Exhibition) in Berlin – which was decisive for the international recognition of the Soviet avant-garde, particularly the Constructivists. A multitalented pioneer in painting, typography, photomontage and

El Lissitzky
**ASNOVA Association
of New Architects**
Prospectus, 1923
Cat.63

exhibition design, Lissiztky personified the modern artist. His visualisation of the poetry of Vladimir Mayakovsky was exemplary. He also published, together with the writer Ilya Ehrenburg, the magazine *Veshch / Gegenstand / Objet* (Object) in Berlin and Moscow. Other progressive artists published their own magazines: for example, Hans Richter and Werner Gräff, *G.-Gestaltung* (D-Design), and Kurt Schwitters, *Merz*. For a number of years these magazines were important connectors between the various avant-garde movements. Personalities like Lissitzky, Tschichold, Schwitters and Theo van Doesburg travelled a great deal throughout Europe teaching and organising exhibitions and conferences, encouraging the exchange of ideas and materials.

■ In Czechoslovakia the work of artists like Karel Teige and Ladislav Sutnar was inspired by the Modernism and utopian politics of Germany and Russia. In Hungary, the artists Farkás Molnár and Lajos Kassák, both connected with the Bauhaus, had a major influence in Central Europe through the avant-garde magazine *MA*. Great creative independence was evident in the works of the Polish artists Henryk Berlewi, Stefan Themerson, Mieczyslaw Szczuka, Tadeuz Peiper and Wladyslaw Strzeminski, which were published in the international magazine *Blok*.

Mieczyslaw Szczuka
and Teresa Zarnower
Europa
**(Poem by Anatol
Stern)**
Booklet, 1929
Cat.124

■ In the meantime the values of the October Revolution of 1917 had become firmly established in the Soviet Union. The Constructivists of Moscow and Leningrad connected their art with the socio-political aims of the Bolshevik vision. Confident of their historical mission, they embraced the notion of progress and politicised the role of the artist, who was to take 'art to the people' in pursuit of a wider collective purpose. The 'Socialist City' – dynamic, noisy and full of simultaneous action – was experienced by this generation as an exciting montage of attractions. In the eyes of these artists the architecture of the printed page was equal to the daring architecture of steel and concrete. The Constructivists perceived the creative act as an act of organisation of material and technical capacities. Revolutionary artists like Alexandr Rodchenko, Varvara Stepanova, Gustav Klucis, Alexei Gan, Solomon Telingater, Nikolai Sidelnikov and others spearheaded the free integration of typography, photography and photomontage. Klucis produced the first Soviet photomontage in 1919. The making of composite images was for him and his contemporaries a means of defining the essence of collective aspirations, to construct a vision of the present with the Socialist future implied.

Anastasia Achtyrko
**VKhUTEMAS /
20 Disciplines**
Design for book cover,
1920
Cat.1

■ The centre for interdisciplinary experiment in the fields of painting, sculpture, architecture and design was the Moscow equivalent to the German Bauhaus – the VKhUTEMAS (Higher State Artistic and Technical Studios). It was the focal point of creative energy where artists could test their ideas under 'laboratory' conditions. The aim was to eliminate the hitherto existing division of art and industrial production. The most influential teacher was Aleksandr Rodchenko who had early on turned his attention towards graphic design, photography and montage. The brothers Georgii and Vladimir Stenberg re-invented the art of the cinema poster (cat.111 and 113, p.55 and cat.112, p.53) combining the compositional rules of Constructivism with the dynamism of cinema. The elements of German functionalism had amalgamated with Constructivism. The introduction of new printing processes like lithography and photogravure enabled Soviet artists to combine the sharp geometry of their typography with powerful, photomontaged imagery. The genres of the photo journal and the illustrated newspaper were imported from Germany and France. A great variety of Soviet illustrated magazines sprang up that reflected current cultural, economic and political trends. The young designers and photographers took this opportunity to transfer their graphic innovations into everyday print. The magazine *SSSR na Stroike* (USSR in Construction), published between 1930 and 1941 in four languages, presented in words and pictures an optimistic propagandistic image of the Soviet Union to the world.

John Heartfield
Hurrah! Armoured Cruiser A is here
Political pamphlet cover, 1928
© The Heartfield Community of Heirs/ VG Bild-Kunst, Bonn and DACS, London 2004
(Not in exhibition, see cat.41)

■ **Photomontage**
The concept of montage – the joining together of hitherto separate elements into a new entity – has its roots in industrial terminology and film editing. Its momentous rise from its roots in cinematography, photography, collage and painting left a legacy of important works of art and design. The formal energy and aesthetic effect of these works had a profound influence on the evolution of Modern art and the development of mass media. The Cubist analysis of the image – the paring down of forms to their basic components – was extended by the precision of photographic observation and the omnipotence of the photo- and cine-camera. The result was the development of a new language of visual communication that could respond swiftly to topical events. This new language was able to unite the hitherto fragmented experiences of technology, war and the city into a new art form that reconciled artists and the public with the jarring and fragmented experience of city life, of industrial dynamism, ideological confrontation and war.

Gustav Klucis
The Reality of our Programme is Active Men and Women – You and I
Design for poster, 1931
Cat.56

■ Photomontage grew from the wish to explore diverse, often fragmented or contradictory, visual information. The compilation of selected image components was based on the perception of simultaneity and the parallelism of opposites. The procedure of cutting and retouching was able to reflect in synthetic images the radical leaps of imagination characteristic of an age of turmoil and utopian idealism. This was particularly well-demonstrated in the works of the inventors of photomontage, John Heartfield in Germany and Gustav Klucis in Russia. It was power over time – the practical capacity to break down the limits between historical time, memory time and event time – which was the true attraction of this new medium.

■ Film editing had turned in the hands of the pioneers of cinema into the art of montage. This process, which transforms film fragments into dramatic components of a motion picture, is similar to the process of montaging still photographs. In both cases photographic images, which in isolation may be seen as trivial, are turned into active elements within a meaningful composite. The inventors of film montage, practitioners and theoreticians, the Soviet filmmakers Dziga Vertov and Sergei Eisenstein, and the German director Walter Ruttmann recognised the latent ambiguity of the film image. They utilised, in the editing process, the image's capacity to retain meaning and to respond to the imposition of additional meaning. The cut from one shot to another stimulates the imagination as it marks the moment of definition, the creation or resolution of a conflict of opposites. The art of constructing intelligible sequences or composites from, at times, randomly gathered materials, is not just the result of more or less skilful manipulation but is first and foremost an intuitive act.

■ The principle of association and dislocation explored in montage surfaced also in the creative thinking of the Surrealists. For them the *objet trouvé* (found object) was the symbol of the accidental, where reality and imagination were fused in dream images, visualisations of the subconscious. Similarly the discovery of visual fragments snatched from everyday life – the inspiring coincidence of splinters of time, the sudden awareness of the potential of a found image – was experienced as a revelation of hidden meanings. The concept of the found image gave artists access to a wealth of materials and the mental tools to tackle the fragmented reality of their time. Like the *objet trouvé*, the image salvaged from anonymity connects with deeper psychological layers, memories or ancient symbols. The intuitive search for meaning in found film and photographic fragments is quite similar to the recognition of the value of the *objet trouvé*, redolent with echoes and suggestions. Only the artist's involvement can animate those latent energies; his sensual response ties him to the object of his desire and focuses his intentions.

■ The creative process of the film- and photomonteur is comprised of six stages:
1. An image stimulates the monteur's curiosity, his tactile and visual memory.
2. The image is then isolated from its original context – the monteur's imagination turns it into material for new work.
3. The image is evaluated for its emotional content and narrative potential, and associations with other images or image components are made.
4. Image components are analysed for their formal, structural or pictorial qualities and they are positioned into a new scale of values.
5. The monteur projects his sympathies or antipathies onto the image and imposes his own cultural or psychological interpretation and determines the further use of the image or its rejection.
6. Images that have thus been tested and evaluated are montaged into a new context.

■ The unity of space and time within the traditional photograph is replaced in montage by an assembly of subjectively selected image elements, which have lost their specific identity but have gained timelessness. Montage produces a heightened experience, in which time and emotion are carefully measured. The ambiguity between object and subject forces the viewer to examine relationships and hierarchies. Photomontage repositions image and content; it alters the perception of reality and multiplies narrative stimuli.

■ The excitement of working with a totally new and untried medium, the affinity between film and photo, the shift of space and time in film and the poetics of manipulated reality in photomontage, were the elements that inspired the avant-garde.

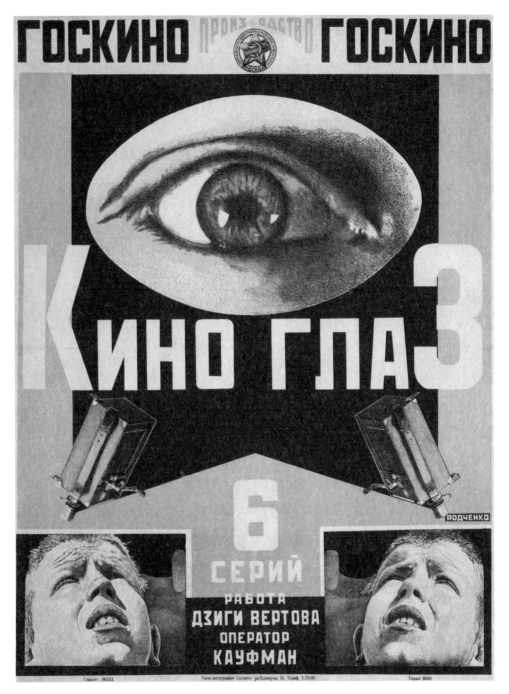

Alexandr Rodchenko
Kino-Eye / Director Dziga Vertov
Poster,1924
Cat.84

Theo van Doesburg
Mécano, No. 3
Journal,1922
(Not in exhibition)

Richard Hollis

Art +Technology = Design

■ Avant-garde artists of the 1920s and 1930s were pioneers of what is now known as 'graphic design'. For more than half a century progressive artists had looked for a new place in an industrialised society. After a search initiated in Victorian England by John Ruskin, continued by William Morris and the Arts and Crafts movement and taken up in Continental Europe in the early twentieth century, avant-garde artists discovered a new role – as designers for the printing industry. They stripped away printers' ornaments and drawn illustrations; they no longer centred headlines and captions on the page; and they brought in abstract, geometrical forms, photographs, plain typefaces and simple lettering, white space and asymmetrical layouts.

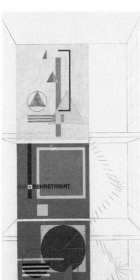

Herbert Bayer
Bauhaus Stairwell
Design for mural,
1923
Cat. 11

■ The slogan 'Art and technology – the new unity' summarised the programme of the Bauhaus school in Germany.[1] The founding director, Walter Gropius, believed that modern painting had 'thrown up countless propositions which are still waiting to be used by the practical world.' The school's driving force became abstract art of the kind imported from the Dutch De Stijl movement and, from Russia, in the form of Contructivism. Contructivism's goals radically extended the ideas of the Arts and Crafts movement. Whereas William Morris had wanted to make art socially useful, the Constructivists aimed for total integration of art and society to the extent that art would disappear. Artists were to work collectively – like scientists in a laboratory – to develop new forms and ultimately to construct a new world. In Germany such ideas had the early support of the Werkbund, an organisation set up in 1907 to foster the co-operation of artists, craftsmen and industry.

■ The Constructivist movement consisted of a small group of artists whose work, based on science and rationality, favoured pure colour and geometric form. Their influence spread across Europe, from Moscow to Rotterdam, as they exchanged ideas through visits, lectures and confrontational exhibitions. They debated with each other at conferences and published their own magazines and manifestos. Some progressive painters abandoned their easels altogether to become full-time designers; others continued painting and considered graphic design work not merely as a source of income, but as an extension of their artistic activity. These artists were, to begin with, as important for formulating certain principles of reform as for the designs that they produced.

■ Manifestos and Programmes
The first significant statement in an assortment of articles and manifestos on graphic design was made by the Hungarian artist Lászlò Moholy-Nagy, who was in charge of the Bauhaus foundation course. His essay, 'Die neue Typographie' (The New Typography), was included in the book accompanying the first public Bauhaus exhibition in 1923 (see Herbert Bayer's poster design for the exhibition, cat. 12, p. 62).[2] Moholy-Nagy began his message with a revolutionary observation: 'Typography is a tool of communication', and he summed up by saying that: 'The new typography is a simultaneous experience of vision and communication.'[2] Moholy-Nagy's attitude to graphic design became increasingly evangelistic and by 1925 he was claiming that: 'The printer's work is part of the foundation on which the NEW world will be built.' He concluded that this new world would find its expression by means of 'typophoto',

a new visual medium using type and photographic images.

What is typography? What is photography? What is typophoto? –

Typography is the communication of ideas through printed design.

Photography is the visual representation of the thing seen.

Typophoto is the most precise visual communication.[3]

Lászlò Moholy-Nagy
Broom Vol.4, No.4
Design for magazine cover, page from Moholy-Nagy's Bauhaus Book, *Painting, Photography, Film*, 1925
© DACS 2004
(Not in exhibition)

■ Moholy-Nagy's integration of the photographic image and type distinguished graphic design from commercial art as it was practised in the advertising studios, where the image – usually a drawn illustration – was put together by a layout artist, or by the printer.

■ At the same time as Moholy-Nagy, the Russian Constructivist artist-architect El Lissitzky was making similar statements: for example, the much-quoted, 'In communicating, the printed word is seen, not heard.'[4] Thanks to Lissitzky, a kind of ambassador for Soviet visual culture, the avant-garde in the east became well-known throughout Europe in the early 1920s. And in his comings and goings to Moscow, Lissitzky took with him and brought back the latest and most progressive examples of new design.

■ Lissitzky's friend, the artist Kurt Schwitters, also played a surprising and critical part in the development of avant-garde graphics. Schwitters was a successful commercial designer in his home-town of Hanover. Among his clients was the city authority: he designed its logo, stationery, and a wide range of forms and publicity material for the education and transport departments and for arts events. Schwitters also published his own magazine, *Merz* – remarkable for its radical layout and its engagement with typographic issues – and was the prime mover

of the Ring neuer Werbegestalter (Circle of New Advertising Designers).

■ The Ring came together in 1927 through meetings and correspondence and Schwitters and the other members planned exhibitions and lectures to convince the public of the effectiveness of the New Typography. Of the Ring's nine original members, seven were abstract painters, self-taught as designers – Willi Baumeister, Max Burchartz, Walter Dexel, César Domela, Robert Michel, Friedrich Vordemberge-Gildewart and Schwitters himself. They were joined by two professionals from the printing industry: Georg Trump and Jan Tschichold. Later members included two Dutch designers, Paul Schuitema and Piet Zwart. Other designers invited to exhibit with the group included Moholy-Nagy and a fellow Hungarian, Lajos Kassák; Ladislav Sutnar and Karel Teige from Czechoslovakia; and, from a new generation of designers, Dick Elffers from Holland, and the Swiss, Max Bill. In the catalogue to accompany an exhibition of the Ring held in Basel in 1929, Schwitters wrote that:

… the advertising designer draws the viewer's attention to what he is advertising, not by means of words, phrases or artificial artistic additions, but simply by designing the printed matter as a unified whole. Unity of the whole means a balance of the graphic elements. The differing values of the various elements create tension. Each element has a weight, a force of a particular strength and with a particular direction. We assess the weight of these forces, which are in tension with one another, so that, when they are added to or subtracted from, the result is zero. Design consists not of the forces themselves, but of balancing them. In printed matter, the forces are the image, lettering, typographic material, printed and unprinted areas, etc., in a state of related tension. Everything in the design is equally important.[5]

■ Other painter-designers harangued the public on the need to reform print design. For instance, Max Burchartz, an Expressionist painter turned Constructivist, addressed professionals in the new commercial art magazine *Gebrauchsgraphik*. In 1924 he set up a design studio in the manufacturing centre of Bochum, Germany. Its name was Werbe-bau (literally, Advertising-Construction). The firm's logo included a square and the logo is included in a Burchartz collage in this book (cat.24, p.73). An A4 leaflet headed 'Publicity Design' set out a programme for Werbe-bau. 'Advertising is the handwriting of every enterprise!', it proclaimed. 'Like handwriting, it shows up a firm's character, its strength and potential.' The leaflet then lays down, following its own recipe for straightforwardness, the requirements of a good advertisement. It must:

1. be objective
2. be clear and concise
3. use modern means
4. have a punchy design
5. be cheap.'[6]

■ In 1926 Werbe-bau's work was used to illustrate an article on advertising by the Hungarian painter-designer Lajos Kassák. Writing in the Swiss Werkbund journal *Das Werk*, he provided the slogan, 'Advertising is constructive art', and concluded the article with typically Constructivist rhetoric: 'To design advertising means to be a social artist.'[7] Kassák also introduced the idea of functionalism: an advertisement was to be judged not as beautiful or as ugly, but as to whether or not it was effective. 'The good advertisement does not analyse or define, it synthesises – a unity of time, content and subject matter. Its fundamental simplicity and clarity make us stop in the street and force us into some decisive response.'

Walter Dexel
'What is the New Typography?'
in *Frankfurter Zeitung*, 5 Febuary 1927
(Not in exhibition)

■ Writing in *Die Form*, the journal of the German Werkbund, Theo van Doesburg, a friend of Kurt Schwitters, also referred to the Werbe-bau leaflet, describing it as exemplary. Van Doesburg, a Dutch painter, one-time Dadaist, poet and theorist, was a central figure in Modern art and design, leader of the De Stijl group, which included Piet Mondrian, and publisher of *De Stijl* magazine. Resident for a time in the Bauhaus' home town of Weimar, Van Doesburg, already experienced in designing for print, provided

a stylistic precedent for what became known as 'Bauhaus' typography. Johannes Molzahn, who attended Van Doesburg's lessons in De Stijl practice, was the first to introduce this style in commercial printing – bold type in capitals, heavy black printers' 'rules' and dots.

Theo van Doesburg
De Stijl, No.9
Cover, 1922
with drawing by
Kasimir Malevich
(Not in exhibition)

■ Van Doesburg was aware of aesthetic developments in Soviet Russia, where artists had found a new kind of visual expression in photomontage. But Van Doesburg was more interested and influenced by the Suprematist theories of geometry introduced by the painter Kasimir Malevich, especially the circle and square, and the diagonal. Van Doesburg invited Lissitzky to contribute to *De Stijl*, and published a Dutch translation of his *Story of Two Squares* (cat.62, p.48). The profound impact that Lissitzky made on Piet Zwart, an associate of the De Stijl group, led to Zwart's uninhibited typographic arrangements (cat.149, p32), his use of photomontage, and an addition to the flow of proclamations: an eight-page essay produced as a printer's A4 brochure, 'From the Old to the New Typography'. It carried a similar message to one of the most articulate manifestos, produced by the Czech critic, collagist and typographer Karel Teige in 1927. Teige's six points are relevant today:

1. Freedom from tradition and prejudice. Eliminating decorativism.
2. Using clearly legible, geometrically simple typefaces.
3. Fulfilling the particular demands of each job.
4. Balancing of space and clear, geometrically organised layout.
5. Exploiting new technologies to create 'typofoto'.
6. Close collaboration of the designer and printer.[8]

■ These self-taught painter-designers were joined by others from the printing industry.

The most enthusiastic of these converts was Jan Tschichold, a calligrapher and typographer from Leipzig, a traditional centre of the printing trade. The 21-year old Tschichold had been inspired by the 1923 Bauhaus exhibition and made himself the most influential spokesman for the New Typography. Two years later he edited the first survey issue of a printing-trade magazine, giving it the title 'Elementare Typographie' (Elemental Typography). Tschichold reprinted many of the avant-garde statements and reproduced his own work alongside examples by his chief influence, Lissitzky, and by the Bauhaus teachers Moholy-Nagy and Herbert Bayer, as well as work by Burchartz, Molzahn and Farkás Molnár.

Farkás Molnár
MA
Design for magazine cover, 1924
Cat.68

■ In both 'Elementare Typographie' and in *Die neue Typographie* (The New Typography), his famous book published in 1928, Tschichold sees abstract painting as the basis for the New Typography. In an account of the avant-garde's typographic experiments in *Die neue Typographie* he describes Dadaist printing – 'its freedom from traditional styles of composition, strong contrasts in type sizes, design and colour, type set at all sorts of angles, all kinds of type, and the use of photography' – and considers it 'utterly untypographic'. In the New Typography, form 'must be created out of function' when 'the function of printed text is communication.'[9] This was the way to 'achieve a typography which expresses the spirit of modern man'. Tschichold went on to codify a mature version of the New Typography published as *Typographische Gestaltung* (Typographic Design) in 1935 in Switzerland after he was driven out of Germany by the Nazis.[10]

■ **Forms of the new graphics**

The most informative contemporary account of the theory and practice of Modernist graphic design was the book *Gefesselter Blick* (Captured Look). Edited by Heinz and Bodo Rasch, and published in Stuttgart in 1930, its introduction is one of the earliest, clearest statements made about graphic design, which it describes as:

> . . . a more or less dense grid of images, like film. Film is function interpreted by images. Text is simply a succession of symbolic signs. Images are basic, supported by signs. As to images, the camera must behave as the viewer's eye, and concentrate attention.[11]

■ The Rasch brothers collected statements and examples of work from 26 artists and designers and included these in their book. Virtually a directory of the avant-garde (with the exception of the Russians) the works included in their book have several common features, which have survived into the graphic design we know today. As one would expect, with few exceptions, the designs are not symmetrical; the type is sanserif; the illustrations are photographs, not drawings. The emphatic stripes, bands and lines typical of early Bauhaus work have been disciplined, and printer's rules have been used for a purpose, especially in tabular lists, to separate one category from another. Technical innovations were later refined: the crude collage of photographs, for example, was transformed into the type of montage where one image dissolved into another. The most common stylistic feature to reappear was the diagonal, inspired by Van Doesburg and frequently employed by the Dutch designers Paul Schuitema (cat.93, p.28) and Piet Zwart (cat.145 and 148, p.32).

Natan Altman
Red Student, **No.8**
Design for journal cover, 1923
Cat.3

■ There are other common features in avant-garde works. For instance, the geometrical forms of Constructivism are pervasive, in particular the square and the circle. The square is sometimes the chief element: in Lissitzky's *Story of Two Squares* (cat.62, p.48), in Hendrikus Wijdeveld's Frank Lloyd Wright exhibition poster (cat.143, p.24), tilted in Natan Altman's designs (cat.3, p.18), and in Herbert Bayer's design for a Bauhaus exhibition poster (cat.12, p.62). The avant-garde intended to dispense with ornament to concentrate on the message of the design. The abstract elements, lines and dots often became embellishments, replacing the printer's traditional decoration.

■ As to text, to begin with, headlines were set all in capitals. Soon the Bauhaus asked, 'since we don't use capital letters when we speak, why should we use them in print?' Without capital letters typesetting could be simplified. So could the typewriter. It was some time before it was realised that capitals were a helpful part of reading. The all-lowercase lettering in the posters by Max Burchartz (cat.23 and cat.25, p.72) and Georg Trump (cat.135, p.21 and cat.136, p.67) is typical of doctrinaire Modernism. More lasting was the exclusive use of sanserif letterforms. In this catalogue, the only appearance of serif letters is in Van Doesburg's cover to *Mécano* (cat.32, p.14), where their historical connotation is Dadaistic and playful. On posters that were printed by lithography, lettering could be drawn freely – as it had been by earlier artists, such as Toulouse-Lautrec. Unless drawn – when it was often given an emphatic geometry – the lettering of avant-garde posters in general followed the forms used in commercial advertisements.

■ **Technology, Photography and Reproduction**
Tschichold stressed the importance of abstract art, but the greatest influence on the new type of printed communication was photography. Moholy-Nagy set out the grammar of a new visual language in his book *Painting, Photography, Film*, first published at the Bauhaus in 1925, and played a large role in *Film und Foto* (Film and Photo), a huge exhibition in Stuttgart arranged by the Werkbund in 1929 (cat.4, p.66). Photography was presented as a new way of seeing and as a mechanical means of objective recording, not as a medium for the pictorial vision of representational painting. The exhibition gave a special section to photomontage which included work by John Heartfield and Soviet designer-photographers.

■ Photography not only provided the images for avant-garde works, it also informed the technology of reproducing these images – by photolithography, by photogravure and in the photoengraving of half-tone blocks. The traditional printing method of letterpress – printing from the raised, inked surface of metal type – was the most common technique for small formats, for books and for most jobbing printing, such as brochures. Large wooden type was made for posters, but the size of image was restricted by the maximum size of a photoengraved block. Simple forms and flat colour were also printed from linocut blocks.

■ The underlying structure of a design printed by letterpress was essentially horizontal-vertical: metal type was produced on a rectangular base (see Moholy-Nagy's Bauhaus-Book brochure [cat.66, p.21] and Georg Trump's poster design [cat.135, p.21]). For printing, the lines of type, in columns, were locked up with spacing material in a rectangular frame – though it was also possible to lock lines of type at an angle. The avant-garde took advantage of this, and they also played with printers' ready-made decorative elements – solid circles (known as bullets), squares, pointing fingers (fists), stars and arrows, and also the straight lengths of wood or metal (rules), to print lines of varying thickness. The posters by Hendrikus Wijdeveld (cat.142, p.25 and cat.143, p.24) are explicitly composed almost entirely of printers' materials.

■ Lithography, developed in the nineteenth century, allowed lettering and text to be combined in the same printing process. Photography made it possible to assemble text and images as film, which could then be transferred to the printing surface. In some cases the design was drawn by the artist directly onto the lithographic stone, as in Raoul Hausmann and Johannes Baader's Dada poster (cat.7, p.8). More often artwork was prepared by the designer and copied by expert draughtsmen at the printers. Their skill in interpreting an original drawing was remarkable: close inspection of a poster often reveals that what appears to be a photograph is in fact a drawn facsimile. Examples are the cinema posters derived from photographic stills by the Stenberg Brothers (cat.111-115. pp.53 and 55) and Mikhail Dlugach (cat.31, p.54).

■ An example of printing by gravure is the photomontage in Lissitzky's 'Russian Exhibition' poster (cat.64, p.49). Whereas in lithography ink is picked up from a flat surface, a stone or zinc plate, in gravure the printing ink, forced into etched images and text, is partly absorbed by the paper. This gives a heavy deposit of ink, and reproduction of photographs without the usual photographic half-tone screen of dots.

■ The most noticeable difference between graphics of the period between the two world wars and today is the absence of full colour in the former, although colour photography was pioneered in Russia well before the First World War. Few of the works in this book are in more than three colours; many are printed only in black and red. For a full-colour effect, designers were ingenious in overprinting two or three colours, and they exploited a traditional printing technique that spread ink of varying colours across the printing press rollers to give a rainbow effect (see Max Bill's poster, cat.19, p.87).

■ For the designer, whatever the printing process, there was little difference in the way finished drawings were prepared. Photographs, drawn illustrations and type had to be stuck onto a heavy white board with instructions on an overlay sheet for photoengraving or platemaking. The airbrush, producing a fine spray, most often of opaque white paint, was used to fade edges of photographs as 'vignettes', to conceal the joins in montages, and to produce cloud effects. The designer had to paint around the outline of cut-out images which were to show no background.

■ Despite the common elements and techniques employed by avant-garde artists in their works, their graphics do not represent 'a style'. The artists shared common attitudes, yet their ways of working were various and inconsistent, and many continued painting as they came to grips with a new world of technology and mass communications. But all of their methods crossed boundaries. Innovations such as the reduction of the image to elementary geometrical forms and the practice of photomontage, for example, appeared in Western Europe and in Russia at the same time. For both professional and political reasons, artists migrated. César Domela, for example, the youngest member of the De Stijl group, worked as a freelance designer in Berlin from 1927 to 1933. And graphic ideas travelled; there is more than an echo of Georg Trump's 1927 poster design (cat.135, p.21) in Rodchenko's cover design for the Soviet magazine *Journalist*, made in 1931 (not in exhibition, p.21).

■ The general public had resisted the innovations of avant-garde artists, and the printing trade was slow to introduce aspects of the New Typography. As the Hitler regime in Germany outlawed the artists as 'degenerate', so there was a return to traditional layout and the most nationalistic styles of 'Gothic' (Fraktur) typefaces. In Russia, artists such as Lissitzky were compelled to make a graphic equivalent of Socialist Realism. Nonetheless, Modernism survived in Europe to resurface in Switzerland at the end of the Second World War, and developed in the United States through the exile of many of its participants, notably Herbert Bayer and Ladislav Sutnar. The legacy of the twentieth-century avant-garde in graphic design can be recognised today: in our newspapers, on billboards, in the branding of corporations and institutions, in our mail-order catalogues, even in the signs on our motorways.

Notes

1. Of the artists in this book, almost all had some contact with or had visited the Bauhaus, apart from the Russians – with the exception of Lissitzky and Malevich. Herbert Bayer, Moholy-Nagy and, for a short time, Mart Stam, taught there; Theo Ballmer, Max Bill and Marianne Brandt were Bauhaus students – but not of graphic design.
2. Moholy-Nagy, Lászlò, 1923, 'Die neue Typographie', translated in Kostelanetz, Richard (ed.), *Moholy-Nagy*, Praeger, New York, 1970, p.75. The word 'typography', used in German, can refer to both text and images.
3. Moholy-Nagy, Lászlò, 'Typo-Photo' in 'Elementare Typographie', special issue of *Typographische Mitteilungen*, October 1925, p.202.
4. Kurt Schwitters quotes these words on the final page of his booklet 'Die Gestaltung in der Typographie' under the heading 'Topography of Typography' (cat.100).
5. Schwitters, Kurt, *Neue Werbegrafik*, exhibition catalogue, Gewerbemuseum, Basel, 1930.
6. Facsimile in *Max Burchartz: Typographische Arbeiten 1924-1931*, Verlag Lars Müller, Baden, 1993.
7. Kassák, Lajos, 'Die Reklame', in *Das Werk*, July 1926, pp.227-228.
8. Teige, Karel, 'Moderni Typo' (1927), quoted in Dluhosch, Eric, and Svacha, Rostislav (eds), *Karel Teige 1900-1951*, MIT Press, Cambridge, Mass. and London, 1999, p.76.8.
9. Tschichold, Jan, *Die neue Typographie*, Leipzig, 1928; reprint, Berlin: Brinkmann & Bose, 1987; English edition, McLean, Ruari (trans.), *The New Typography*, University of California Press, Berkeley and Los Angeles, 1995, p.56.
10. Tschichold, Jan, *Typographische Gestaltung*, Benno Schwabe, Basel, 1935; English edition: McLean, Ruari (trans.), *Asymmetric Typography*, Faber & Faber, London, 1967.
11. Rasch, Heinz and Rasch, Bodo (eds.), *Gefesselter Blick*, Stuttgart: Wissenschaftlicher Verlag Dr Zaugg, 1930; reprint, Lars Müller, Baden, 1996.

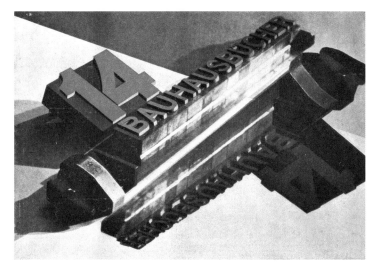

László Moholy-Nagy
14 Bauhaus Books
Catalogue,1927
Cat.66

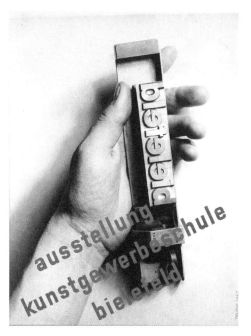

Alexandr Rodchenko
Journalist
Magazine cover,1930
© DACS 2004
(Not in exhibition)

Georg Trump
**Exhibition / School of Applied Arts /
Bielefeld**
Design for poster,1927
Cat.135

Kurt Schwitters and Theo van Doesburg
Little Dada Soirée
Poster,1923
Cat.101

50 ARCHITECTEN VAN
INTERNATIONALE
BEKENDHEID HEBBEN
298 ONTWERPEN VAN
ZAKELIJKE „FANTASIELOOZE"
ARCHITECTUUR
TEZAMEN GEBRACHT
DE VEREENIGING
„OPBOUW" TE R'DAM
ORGANISEERT EEN
TENTOONSTELLING
IN REST. „DE LA PAIX"
COOLSINGEL 103 - R'DAM
VAN 5 TOT 28 APRIL
GEOP. 10-17 EN 19-22 UUR

Mart Stam
International Architecture Exhibition / Rotterdam
Poster, 1928
Cat. 110

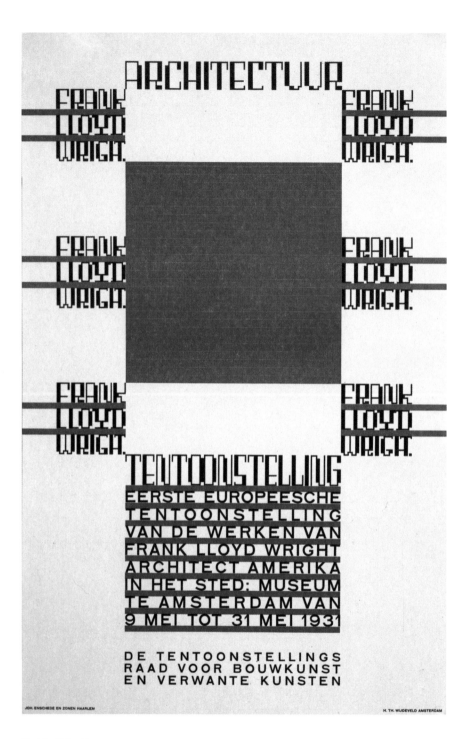

Hendrikus Wijdeveld
Architecture Exhibition / Frank Lloyd Wright
Poster, 1931
Cat. 143

Hendrikus Wijdeveld
International Economic-Historical
Exhibition / Amsterdam
Poster, 1929
Cat. 142

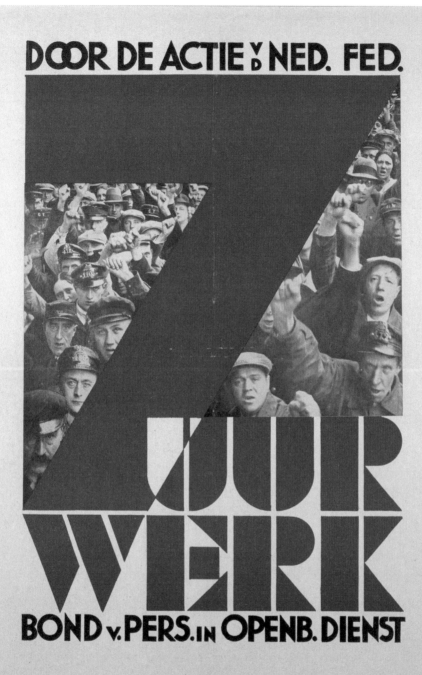

Anon
7 Hours Work
Poster, *c.*1930
Cat.5

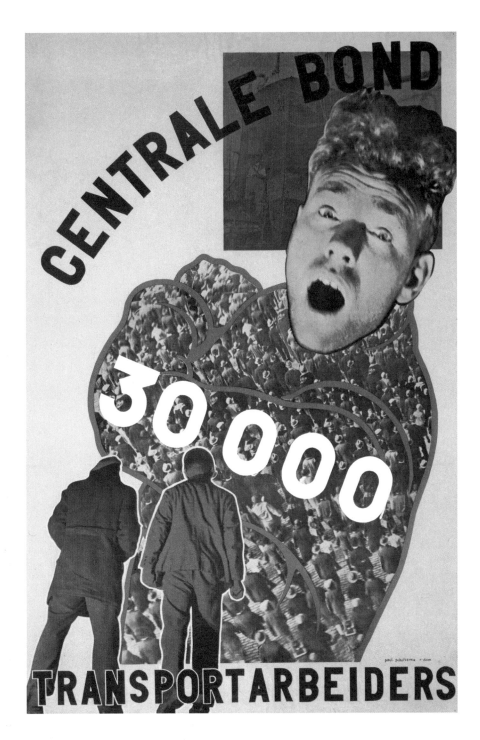

Paul Schuitema
Central Union of 30,000 Transport Workers
Poster, 1930
Cat. 96

Paul Schuitema
Every Berkel is a Proved Machine
Weighing machines advertisement, 1926
Cat.93

Paul Schuitema
Toledo Berkel 85000
Weighing machine advertisement, 1926
Cat.95

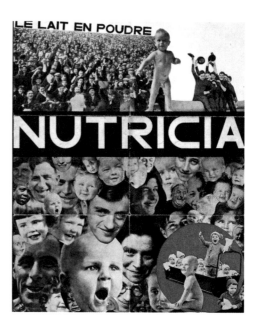

Paul Schuitema
Nutricia Milk Powder
Poster, c.1926
Cat.94

Fré Cohen
Amsterdam Sea and Airport
Prospectus, *c*.1932
Cat.27

Fré Cohen
Schiphol Airport
Prospectus, *c*.1932
Cat.28

Hendrik Nicolaas Werkman
The Next Call, No.7
Magazine,1926
Cat.140

Hendrik Nicolaas Werkman
The Next Call, No.8
Magazine,1926
Cat.141

Piet Zwart
Verloop Estate Agents
Poster, 1923
Cat. 144

Piet Zwart
Trio Printers
Page from booklet, 1931
Cat. 149

Piet Zwart
NKF Paper Insulation
Advertisement, 1925
Cat. 146

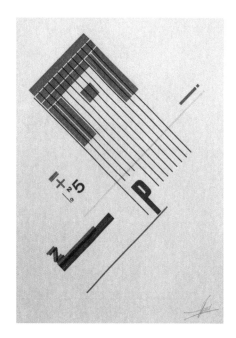

Piet Zwart
Homage to a Young Woman
Typographic experiment, 1925
Cat. 145

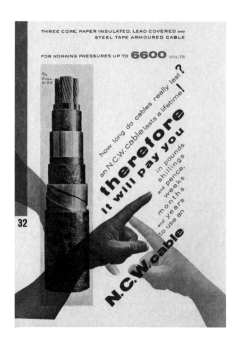

Piet Zwart
N.C.W. Cable
Catalogue, 1926
Cat. 147

Piet Zwart
International Exhibition of Film / The Hague
Poster, 1928
Cat. 148

Vasilii Elkin
**Long Live the Red Army – the Armed Detachment
of the Proletarian Revolution!**
Design for poster, c.1933
Cat.36

Vasilii Elkin
Production
Design for book cover, *c.*1932
Cat.35

Vasilii Ermilov
Workers' Library
Design for prospectus, *c.*1930
Cat.38

Alexei Gan
First Exhibition of Contemporary Architecture
Poster,1927
Cat.39

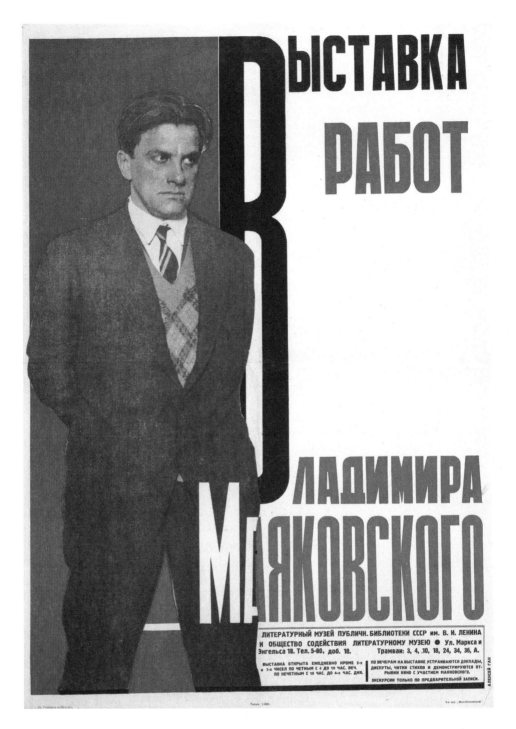

Alexei Gan
Vladimir Mayakovsky / Twenty Years of Work
Exhibition poster, 1930
Cat. 40

Gustav Klucis
Electrification of the Entire Country
Photomontage,1920
Cat.51

Gustav Klucis
Towards a World October
Design for poster,1931
Cat.57

Gustav Klucis
Plan for the Socialist Offensive of 1929-30
Design,1929
Cat.52

Gustav Klucis
**The Reality of our Programme is
Active Men and Women – You and I**
Poster,1931
Cat.55

Gustav Klucis
**The Development of Transport / One of the Important
Tasks for the Implementation of the Five-Year Plan**
Poster, 1929
Cat. 53

Valentina Kulagina
**International Women Workers Day /
The Review of Socialist Achievements**
Poster,1930
Cat.59

Natalia Pinus-Bucharova
**Women Workers Participate Actively
in a Life of Productivity and Social Peace!**
Poster, 1933
Cat. 76

Борьба за политехническую школу есть борьба за пятилетну,
за кадры, за классовое коммунистическое воспитание

Elizavieta Ignatovich
**The Struggle for the Polytechnics is
the Struggle for the Five-Year Plan, for
the Cadre and a Communist Education**
Poster,1931
Cat.49

Varvara Stepanova and Boris Ignatovitch
Strengthen the Defence with Whatever You Can
Design for book cover, c.1934
Cat.116

Vasilii Ermilov
Ukrainian Exhibition of Books and Print
Poster (proof),1927
Cat.37

Liubov Popova
The Magnanimous Cuckold, Actor No.7
Costume design,1921
Cat.78

Liubov Popova
**Long Live the Dictatorship
of the Proletariat!**
Design for poster, 1921
Cat. 77

Varvara Stepanova
Tarelkin's Death / Meyerhold Theatre
Poster, 1922
Cat. 114

El Lissitzky
Story of Two Squares
Book,1922
Cat.62

El Lissitzky and Vladimir Mayakovsky
For the Voice
Book,1923
Cat.65

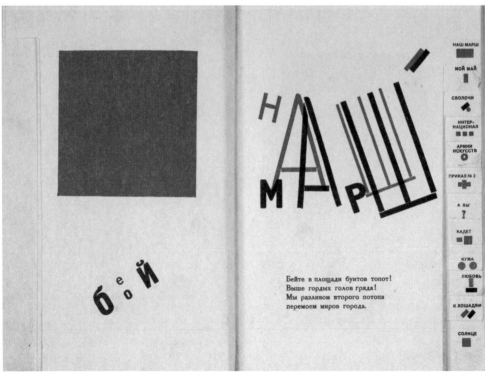

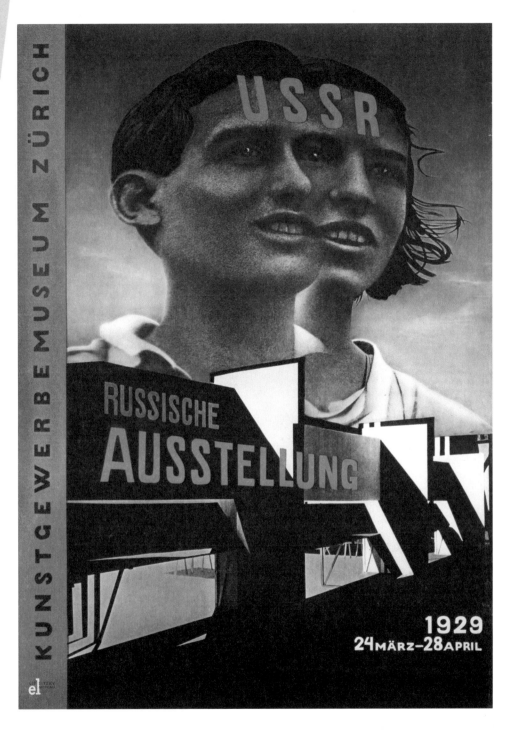

El Lissitzky
USSR / Russian Exhibition / Zurich
Poster,1929
Cat.64

Alexandr Rodchenko
LEF, No.2
Prospectus, 1924
Cat.85

Alexandr Rodchenko
LEF, No.3
Design for magazine cover, 1924
Cat.86

Alexandr Rodchenko
**A Man Needs a Watch /
A Watch from Mozer /
Mozer only at GUM**
Advertisement, 1923
Cat.81

Alexandr Rodchenko
Shame on You
Your Name is not yet on the List of Shareholders
Get Dobrolet Shares
Poster, 1923
Cat. 82

Nikolai Prusakov
The Second Exhibition of Film Posters
Poster, 1926
Cat. 79

Vladimir Stenberg and Georgii Stenberg
Symphony of a Great City /
Director Walter Ruttmann
Film poster,1928
Cat.112

Mikhail Dlugach
Cement / **Director Vladimir B Vilner**
Film poster, 1928
Cat. 31

Vladimir Stenberg and Georgii Stenberg
High Society Wager / **Director Carl Froelich**
Film poster,1927
Cat.111

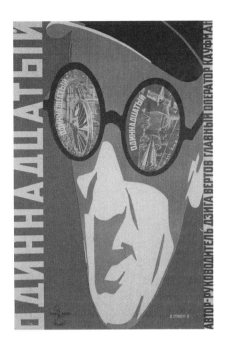

Vladimir Stenberg and Georgii Stenberg
The Eleventh Year / **Director Dziga Vertov**
Film poster,1928
Cat.113

Nikolai Prusakov
The Ranks of Men / **Director Yakov Protazanov**
Film poster,1929
Cat.80

Anton Lavinsky
Strike / **Director Sergei Eisenstein**
Film poster,1925
Cat.60

Nikolai Sidelnikov
Advertising Technique, No.2
Design for magazine cover, c.1930
Cat.102

Nikolai Sidelnikov
Untitled (#92)
Photomontage, c.1930
Cat.109

Nikolai Sidelnikov
The Time, the Energy, the Will
Photomontage, c.1930
Cat.104

Nikolai Sidelnikov
Bicycle Sport
Design for book cover, c.1930
Cat.103

Nikolai Sidelnikov
Untitled (#71)
Photomontage, *c.*1930
Cat.108

Solomon Telingater
Kirsanov has the Floor
Book cover, 1930
Cat. 134

Solomon Telingater
Stretching
Collage, *c.*1929
Cat.133

Solomon Telingater
Theatre of the Red Army
Design for poster, 1928/29
Cat. 132

Solomon Telingater
Ten Posters of Exercise and Sports 1
Design for poster, 1928/29
Cat. 128

Solomon Telingater
Ten Posters of Exercise and Sports 2
Design for poster, 1928/29
Cat. 129

Solomon Telingater
Ten Posters of Exercise and Sports 3
Design for poster, 1928/29
Cat. 130

Solomon Telingater
Ten Posters of Exercise and Sports 4
Design for poster, 1928/29
Cat. 131

Karl Peter Röhl
Constructivist Exhibition / Weimar
Poster, 1923
Cat. 89

Herbert Bayer
State Bauhaus Exhibition / Weimar
Design for poster, 1923
Cat. 12

Herbert Bayer
Exhibition of European Applied Arts / Leipzig
Poster, 1927
Cat. 13

Herbert Bayer
German Section / Exhibition of the Society of Decorative
Artists / Paris
Poster, 1930
Cat. 15

Willi Baumeister
The Home / Werkbund Exhibition / Stuttgart
Poster,1927
Cat.10

Anon
Film and Photo / International Exhibition / Stuttgart
Poster, 1929
Cat. 4

Georg Trump
The Photographic Image
Poster, 1930
Cat. 136

Marianne Brandt
Sport
Photomontage, 1928
Cat.22

Marianne Brandt
Our American Sisters
Photomontage, 1928
Cat.21

César Domela
Fotomontage / State Museum Berlin
Exhibition catalogue, 1931
Cat.34

Walter Dexel
Contemporary Photography Exhibition / Magdeburg
Poster,1929
Cat.30

John Heartfield
The Last Piece of Bread
Poster, 1932
Cat. 45

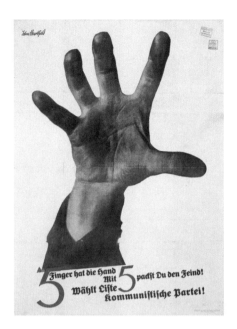

John Heartfield
The Hand has 5 Fingers, With 5 You Grab the Enemy!
Poster, 1928
Cat. 43

John Heartfield
No Man, No Penny for Capitalist War Arms
Poster, 1928
Cat. 42

John Heartfield
Join Our Struggle! Vote Communist, List 4
Poster, 1930
Cat. 44

John Heartfield
Hurray! The Battle Cruiser has Arrived!
Photomontage,1927
Cat.41

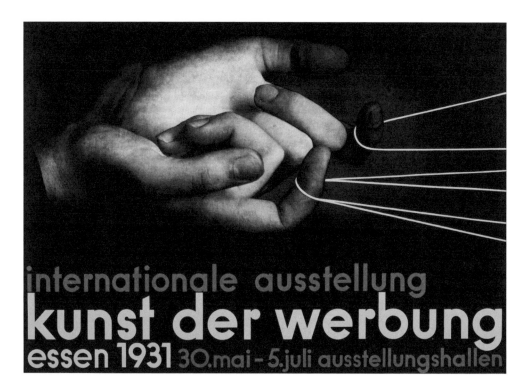

Max Burchartz
Art of Advertising / International Exhibition / Essen
Poster, 1931
Cat. 25

Max Burchartz
Dance Festival / Essen
Poster, 1928
Cat. 23

Max Burchartz and Johannis Canis
Bochum Union
Mining equipment and foundry catalogue,
1929
Cat.26

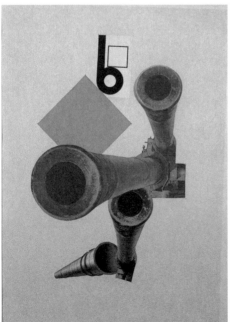

Max Burchartz
Red Square
Collage, c.1928
Cat.24

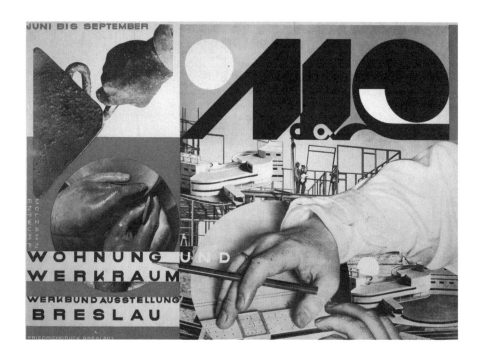

Johannes Molzahn
Home and Workspace Exhibition / Breslau
Poster,1928
Cat.70

Johannes Molzahn
Home and Workspace Exhibition / Breslau
Poster,1929
Cat.71

74 Germany

Johannes Molzahn
Central German Crafts Exhibition / Magdeburg
Poster,1925
Cat.69

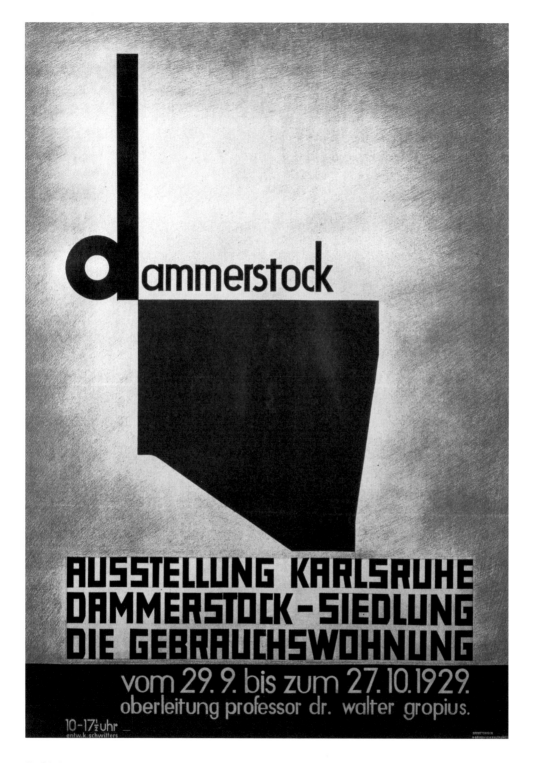

Kurt Schwitters
Dammerstock / Exhibition of Housing / Karlsruhe
Poster, 1929
Cat. 99

F₁ GESETZE DER BILD-FORM	GESETZE DER BILD-FORM F₁
ORIENTIERUNG.	**WERBUNG.**

ruhend		bewegt	
ohne Mitte	daher ausgeglichen	betonte Mitte	daher ausstrahlend
passiv		aktiv	
objektiv		subjektiv	
senkrecht - wagerecht -	Vierecke	parallel oder schräg,	alle beliebigen Formen
Teile gleichartig, das Negativ jeden Teiles ist im Wesen gleich seinem Positiv		Teile verschiedenartig. Negativ und Positiv sind wesentlich verschieden, wie konvex und konkav	
also - orientierend		also - werbend	aggressiv
10			11

Kurt Schwitters
New Typographic Design
Booklet,1930
Cat.100

Kurt Schwitters
Merz = Kurt Schwitters
Poster,1923
Cat.98

Jan Tschichold
The Woman Without a Name, Part Two /
Director Georg Jacoby
Film poster, 1928
Cat. 138

Jan Tschichold
The Trousers / Director Hans Behrendt
Film poster, 1927
Cat. 137

Henryk Berlewi
First Exhibition of Mechano-Faktur
Design for poster, 1924
Cat. 18

Henryk Berlewi
Neo Faktur 23
Design, 1923
Cat. 17

Wladyslaw Strzemiński
From Beyond
Book,1930
Cat.117

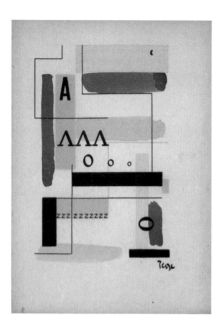

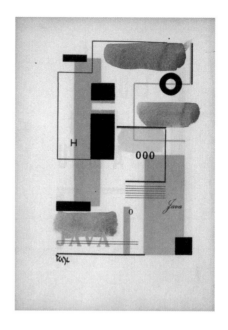

Karel Teige
Fragment (a)
Reworked page from book by K. Biebl
*With a Ship Importing Tea and Coffee,*1928
Cat.125

Karel Teige
Fragment (b)
Reworked page from book by K. Biebl
*With a Ship Importing Tea and Coffee,*1928
Cat.126

VÝSTAVNÍ SÍNĚ ÚSTŘ. KNIHOVNY HLAV. MĚSTA PRAHY
(Marianské náměstí)

Belgie • ČSR • Francie • Holandsko • Italie • Německo Rakousko • S S S R • Švýcary • USA

M**VÝSTAVA**
EZINÁRODNÍ NOVÉ
A**RCHITEKTURY**

Putovní výstava říšskoněmeckého Werkbundu a soubor československé architektury

Pořádá:
KLUB ARCHITEKTŮ
(„STAVBA")

Pod protektorátem p. ministra veřejných prací Dra Spiny a ministra národní osvěty Dra Štefanka

Otevřena od 16.–31./V., denně od 9–18 h. – **Vstup 4 Kč, studenti a dělníci 2 Kč**

Karel Teige
International Exhibition of New Architecture
Poster,1929
Cat.127

Ladislav Sutnar
The Minimal House
Booklet, 1933
Cat. 123

Ladislav Sutnar
Motorist and the Law
Book cover, 1932
Cat. 121

Ladislav Sutnar
Exhibition of Modern Trade / Brno
Poster,1929
Cat.118

Ladislav Sutnar
**International Exhibition of Toys
and Educational Materials**
Poster, c.1930
Cat.120

Ladislav Sutnar
Exhibition of the Harmonious Home
Poster,1930
Cat.119

GEBR. FRETZ AG. ZÜRICH

kunsthaus zürich
abstrakte und
surrealistische malerei
und plastik

6. oktober bis 3. november 1929 täglich geöffnet 10-12 und 2-5 montags geschlossen

Jean Arp and Walter Cyliax
**Abstract and Surrealist Painting
and Sculpture / Zurich**
Poster, 1929
Cat. 6

86 Switzerland

Theo Ballmer
Hundred Years of Photography / Exhibition at the
Museum of Applied Arts / Basel
Poster, 1927
Cat. 8

Theo Ballmer
International Office Exhibition / Basel
Poster, 1928
Cat. 9

Max Bill
Relâche / Ariadne / Dance Studio Wulff
Poster, 1931
Cat. 19

Switzerland 87

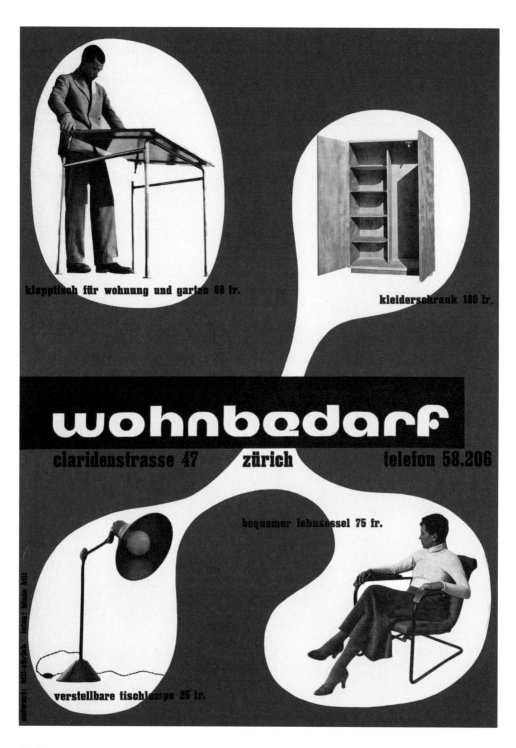

Max Bill
Wohnbedarf Home Furnishings Store
Poster, 1932
Cat. 20

Jan Tschichold
Constructivists / Kunsthalle Basel
Exhibition poster, 1937
Cat. 139

List of Works

All measurements are height × width

Page references are to illustrations in this book

All works are courtesy the Merrill C. Berman Collection

■ **Anastasia Achtyrko**
(1902-1968)
USSR

1 / p.10
**VKhUTEMAS /
20 Disciplines** 1920
Design for book cover: gouache, ink, pencil
23 × 18.7 cm

■ **Natan Altman** (1899-1970)
USSR

2 / Not illustrated
Red Student, **No.1**
1923
Design for journal cover: ink, crayon
39.2 × 29 cm

3 / p.18
Red Student, **No.8**
1923
Design for journal cover: ink, gouache
39.2 × 29 cm
© DACS 2004 / Photo: Mike Fear

■ **Anon**
Germany

4 / p.66
**Film and Photo /
International Exhibition /
Stuttgart** 1929
Poster: lithograph
83.8 × 58.8 cm

■ **Anon**
The Netherlands

5 / p.26
7 Hours Work *c.*1930
Poster: lithograph
55.2 × 40.2 cm

■ **Jean Arp** (1886-1966)
and **Walter Cyliax** (1899-1945)
Switzerland

6 / p.86
**Abstract and Surrealist
Painting and Sculpture /
Zurich** 1929
Exhibition poster: lithograph
128.3 × 90.5 cm

■ **Johannes Baader**
(1876-1955)
and **Raoul Hausmann**
(1886-1971)
Germany

7 / p.8
Dada Milky Way 1918
Poster: lithograph, ink
50.2 x 30.5 cm
© ADAGP, Paris and DACS, London 2004

■ **Theo Ballmer** (1902-1965)
Switzerland

8 / p.87
**Hundred Years of
Photography / Exhibition
at the Museum of Applied
Arts / Basel** 1927
Poster: lithograph
124.5 × 90.2 cm

9 / p.87
**International Office
Exhibition / Basel** 1928
Poster: lithograph
127 × 90.4 cm

■ **Willi Baumeister**
(1889-1955)
Germany

10 / p.65
**The Home / Werkbund
Exhibition / Stuttgart** 1927
Poster: lithograph
104.5 × 81.8 cm
© DACS 2004

■ **Herbert Bayer** (1900-1985)
Germany

11 / p.15
Bauhaus Stairwell 1923
Design for mural: gouache, pencil, cut paper
59 × 26.4 cm
© DACS 2004

12 / p.62
**State Bauhaus Exhibition /
Weimar** 1923
Design for poster: ink, pencil, gouache
43 × 30.2 cm
© DACS 2004

13 / p.63
**Exhibition of European
Applied Arts / Leipzig** 1927
Poster: lithograph
89.7 × 59.5 cm
© DACS 2004

14 / Not illustrated
**Ventzky Agricultural
Machinery** 1928
Design for exhibition stand: pencil, gouache, halftone photograph
49 × 67.5 cm

15 / p.64
**German Section / Exhibition
of the Society of Decorative
Artists / Paris** 1930
Poster: lithograph
158.2 × 117.3 cm
© DACS 2004

■ **Henryk Berlewi** (1894-1967)
Poland

16 / Not illustrated
Mechano Faktur 1923
Design: gouache
54.2 × 43.2 cm

17 / p.80
Neo Faktur 23
1923
Design: gouache, pencil
55 × 44 cm

18 / p.80
**First Exhibition of
Mechano-Faktur** 1924
Design for poster: gouache
63.5 × 50.2 cm

■ **Max Bill** (1908-1994)
Switzerland

19 / p.87
**Relâche / Ariadne / Dance
Studio Wulff** 1931
Poster: letterpress
64.3 × 91 cm
© DACS 2004

20 / p.88
**Wohnebedarf Home
Furnishings Store** 1932
Poster: letterpress
128 × 90.5 cm
© DACS 2004

■ **Marianne Brandt**
(1893-1983)
Germany

21 / p.68
Our American Sisters 1928
Photomontage: halftone photographs, printed letters, hand lettering
49.7 × 31.1 cm
© DACS 2004

22 / p.68
Sport 1928
Photomontage: halftone photographs, printed letters
48.2 × 31.1 cm
© DACS 2004

■ **Max Burchartz** (1887-1961)
Germany

23 / p.72
Dance Festival / Essen 1928
Poster: lithograph
89.8 × 83.6 cm
© DACS 2004 / Photo: Mike Fear

24 / p.73
Red Square, *c.*1928
Collage: gouache, halftone photograph, printed logo
51.8 × 35.2 cm
© DACS 2004

25 / p.72
**Art of Advertising /
International Exhibition /
Essen** 1931
Poster: lithograph
59 × 83 cm
© DACS 2004

■ **Max Burchartz**
and **Johannes Canis**
Germany

26 / p.73
Bochum Union 1929
Mining equipment and
foundry catalogue:
lithograph
29.8 × 21.6 cm
© DACS 2004

■ **Fré Cohen** (1903-1943)
The Netherlands

27 / p.29
Amsterdam Sea and Airport
c.1932
Prospectus: lithograph
24 × 15.7 cm (open)
By courtesy of the Fré Cohen Estate.
The Hague, Netherlands

28 / p.29
Schiphol Airport c.1932
Prospectus: lithograph
18.4 × 33.3 cm (open)
By courtesy of the Fré Cohen Estate.
The Hague, Netherlands

■ **Walter Dexel** (1890-1973)
Germany

29 / Not illustrated
**Gas for Cooking, Baking,
Heating, Lighting** 1924
Design for illuminated sign:
ink, gouache, pencil, cut
paper, hand lettering
50.2 × 34 cm

30 / p.69
**Contemporary Photography
Exhibition / Magdeburg** 1929
Poster: linocut
83.8 × 59.4 cm

■ **Mikhail Dlugach**
(1893-1989)
USSR

31 / p.54
Cement / Director
Vladimir B Vilner 1928
Film poster: lithograph
106.5 × 70.5 cm

■ **Theo van Doesburg**
(1883-1931)
The Netherlands

32 / Not illustrated
Mécano, **No.3**
1922
Journal: letterpress
16.5 × 12.8 cm

33 / Not illustrated
**Six Years / NB De Stijl /
Dada 1923**
1923
Postcard: ink, watercolour,
stamped and printed letters
8.3 × 13.7 cm

■ **César Domela** (1900-1992)
Netherlands / Germany

34 / p.68
**Fotomontage / State
Museum Berlin** 1931
Exhibition catalogue:
letterpress
21 × 14.6 cm
© ADAGP, Paris and DACS, London 2004

■ **Vasilii Elkin** (1897-1991)
USSR

35 / p.35
Production c.1932
Design for book cover:
halftone photos, printed
letters, pencil, cut paper
55.9 × 41.9 cm

36 / p.34
**Long Live the Red Army –
the Armed Detachment of
the Proletarian Revolution!**
c.1933
Design for poster: gelatin
silver print with gouache
28.8 × 21 cm

■ **Vasilii Ermilov** (1894-1968)
USSR

37 / p.45
**Ukrainian Exhibition of
Books and Print** 1927
Poster (proof):
woodblock
98 × 71.7 cm

38 / p.35
Workers' Library c.1930
Design for prospectus:
photomontage, gouache, ink
27 × 41.1 cm

■ **Alexei Gan** (1889-1942)
USSR

39 / p.36
**First Exhibition of
Contemporary Architecture**
1927
Poster: letterpress
106.5 × 70.5 cm

40 / p.37
**Vladimir Mayakovsky /
Twenty Years of Work** 1930
Exhibition poster: lithograph
64.8 × 46 cm

■ **John Heartfield** (1891-1968)
Germany

41 / p.71
**Hurray! The Battle Cruiser
has Arrived!** 1927
Photomontage: gelatin silver
print
21 × 15.5 cm
© The Heartfield Community of Heirs/
VG Bild-Kunst, Bonn and DACS, London
2004

42 / p.70
**No Man, No Penny for
Capitalist War Arms** 1928
Poster: lithograph
71.2 × 47 cm
© The Heartfield Community of Heirs/
VG Bild-Kunst, Bonn and DACS, London
2004

43 / p.70
**The Hand has 5 Fingers,
With 5 You Grab the Enemy!**
1928
Poster: lithograph
100.4 × 74 cm
© The Heartfield Community of Heirs/
VG Bild-Kunst, Bonn and DACS, London
2004

44 / p.70
**Join Our Struggle! Vote
Communist, List 4** 1930
Poster: lithograph
70.2 × 50 cm
© The Heartfield Community of Heirs/
VG Bild-Kunst, Bonn and DACS, London
2004

45 / p.70
The Last Piece of Bread 1932
Poster: lithograph
95 × 71.5 cm
© The Heartfield Community of Heirs/VG
Bild-Kunst, Bonn and DACS, London 2004

■ **Hannah Höch** (1889-1978)
Germany

46 / Not illustrated
**Spring Fair of the Crafts
Association** c.1925
Exhibition poster: lithograph
35.9 × 47.3 cm

■ **Vilmos Huszar** (1884-1960)
The Netherlands

47 / Not illustrated
Boulevard St. Michel 1927
Design: lithograph
36.8 × 45.7 cm

48 / Not illustrated
**Exhibition of Contemporary
Applied Art** 1929
Poster: lithograph
69.9 × 59.7 cm

■ **Elizavieta Ignatovich**
(1903-1983)
USSR

49 / p.44
**The Struggle for the
Polytechnics is the Struggle
for the Five-Year Plan, for
the Cadre and a Communist
Education** 1931
Poster: letterpress,
lithograph
52 × 72 cm

■ **Lajos Kassák** (1887-1967)
Hungary

50 / Not illustrated
Mentor / Modern Graphics
c.1928
Advertisement: lithograph
24.8 × 18.8 cm

■ **Gustav Klucis** (1895-1938)
USSR

51 / p.38
**Electrification of the Entire
Country** 1920
Photomontage: ink, gouache,
gelatin silver prints,
coloured
paper, pencil, printed letters
46 × 27.5 cm

52 / p.39
**Plan for the Socialist
Offensive of 1929-30** 1929
Design: gelatin silver prints,
gouache, printed letters
48.5 × 35 cm

53 / p.41
**The Development
of Transport / One of
the Important Tasks for
the Implementation of
the Five-Year Plan** 1929
Poster: lithograph
73.2 × 51 cm

54 / Not illustrated
**Let us Repay our Coal Debt
to the Nation!** 1930
Poster: lithograph
143.5 × 103 cm

55 / p.40
**The Reality of our
Programme is Active Men
and Women – You and I** 1931
Poster: lithograph
142.4 × 103.5 cm

56 / p.11
**The Reality of our
Programme is Active Men
and Women – You and I** 1931
Design for poster: gelatin
silver prints, ink, gouache,
photographed letters
24.4 × 35.6 cm

57 / p.39
Towards a World October
1931
Design for poster: gelatin
silver prints, halftone
photographs, gouache, ink
28.2 × 20.5 cm

■ **Valentina Kulagina**
(1902-1987)
USSR

58 / Not illustrated
We are Building 1929
Design: watercolour,
gouache, sandpaper, halftone
photographs, cut paper
56.8 × 36.2 cm

59 / p.42
**International Women
Workers Day / The Review of
Socialist Achievements** 1930
Poster: lithograph
108.9 × 72.1 cm
Photo: Mike Fear

■ **Anton Lavinsky** (1893-1968)
USSR

60 / p.55
*Strike / Director Sergei
Eisenstein* 1925
Film poster: lithograph
106.7 × 70.8 cm
© DACS 2004

■ **Bart van der Leck**
(1876-1958)
Netherlands

61 / p.8
Delft Salad Oil 1919
Design for poster:
gouache, pencil
89.2 × 61 cm
© DACS 2004

■ **El Lissitzky** (1890-1941)
USSR

62 / p.48
Story of Two Squares 1922
Book: letterpress
28 × 22.4 cm
© DACS 2004

63 / p.9
**ASNOVA Association of New
Architects** 1923
Magazine cover: letterpress
35.7 × 26.7 cm
© DACS 2004

64 / p.49
**USSR / Russian Exhibition /
Zurich** 1929
Poster: photogravure,
lithograph
126.5 × 90.5 cm
© DACS 2004

■ **El Lissitzky** and
Vladimir Mayakovsky
(1893-1930)
USSR

65 / p.48
For the Voice 1923
Book: letterpress
19 × 13.5 cm
© DACS 2004

■ **Lászlò Moholy-Nagy**
(1895-1946)
Germany

66 / p.21
14 Bauhaus Books 1927
Catalogue: letterpress
15 × 21 cm
© DACS 2004

67 / Not illustrated
Erwin Piscator / *Political
Theatre* 1930
Book (Spanish edition):
letterpress
22.2 × 16.2 cm

■ **Farkás Molnár** (1897-1945)
Hungary

68 / p.18
MA 1924
Design for magazine cover:
gouache, ink, pencil, cut paper
30.6 × 30.8 cm

■ **Johannes Molzahn**
(1895-1965)
Germany

69 / p.75
**Central German Crafts
Exhibition / Magdeburg** 1925
Poster: lithograph
86.8 × 62 cm

70 / p.74
**Home and Workspace
Exhibition / Breslau** 1928
Poster: lithograph
60 × 85.6 cm

71 / p.74
**Home and Workspace
Exhibition / Breslau** 1929
Poster: lithograph
60 × 85.5 cm

■ **Oskar Nerlinger** (1893-1969)
Germany

72 / Not illustrated
Construction 1922
Collage: cardboard on
card
32.7 × 24.1 cm

73 / Not illustrated
Construction Town 1922
Design: gouache on card
32.7 × 22.9 cm

■ **Josef Peeters** (1895-1960)
Belgium

74 / Not illustrated
Hurray! 19th May, 1921 1921
Design for poster: gouache
and collage
47.6 × 37.5 cm

75 / Not illustrated
**We are Building / In
Anticipation of 19th May,
1924** 1924
Design for poster: gouache
47.3 × 37.3 cm

■ **Natalia Pinus-Bucharova**
(1901-1986)
USSR

76 / p.43
**Women Workers Participate
Actively in a Life of
Productivity and Social
Peace!** 1933
Poster: lithograph
97.5 × 70cm

■ **Liubov Popova** (1889-1924)
USSR

77 / p.47
**Long Live the Dictatorship of
the Proletariat!** 1921
Design for poster: ink, watercolour, pencil, cut paper
20.1 × 24.9 cm

78 / p.46
The Magnanimous Cuckold,
Actor No.7 1921
Costume design: pencil,
gouache, cut paper
32.6 × 23.2 cm

■ **Nikolai Prusakov**
(1900-1952)
USSR

79 / p.52
**The Second Exhibition
of Film Posters** 1926
Poster: lithograph
108.3 × 71.1 cm

80 / p.55
The Ranks of Men / Director
Yakov Protazanov 1929
Film poster: lithograph
94 × 62.2 cm

■ **Alexandr Rodchenko**
(1891-1956)
USSR

81 / p.50
**A Man Needs a Watch /
A Watch from Mozer /
Mozer only at GUM** 1923
Advertisement: letterpress
18 × 15.4 cm
© DACS 2004

82 / p.51
**Shame on You
Your Name is not yet
on the List of Shareholders
Get Dobrolet Shares** 1923
Poster: lithograph
70.2 × 51.5 cm
© DACS 2004

83 / Not illustrated
**Dobrolet / Every one,
Every one** 1923
Poster: lithograph
34.9 × 45.1 cm

84 / p.13
Kino-Eye / Director Dziga
Vertov 1924
Poster: lithograph
91.5 × 68 cm
© DACS 2004

85 / p.50
LEF, **No.2** 1924
Prospectus: letterpress
23.3 × 15.5 cm
© DACS 2004

86 / p.50
LEF, **No.3** 1924
Design for magazine cover:
gelatin silver prints, printed
letters, cut paper letters, hand
lettering, pencil, gouache,
coloured paper
23.2 × 14.5 cm
© DACS 2004

87 / Not illustrated
Look *c.*1924
Advertising bookmark:
gouache on board
13.5 × 13 cm

■ **Alexandr Rodchenko**
and **Vladimir Mayakovsky**
USSR

88 / Not illustrated
Give me Sun at Night 1923
Design for poster: gouache,
ink, pencil, gelatin silver print
11.2 × 28.6 cm

■ **Karl Peter Röhl** (1890-1975)
Germany

89 / p.62
**Constructivist Exhibition /
Weimar** 1923
Poster: lithograph
92.3 × 59 cm
Photo: Mike Fear

■ **Oskar Schlemmer**
(1888-1943)
Germany

90 / p.9
The Triadic Ballet 1922
Poster: lithograph
82.5 × 56 cm
© 2004 / The Oskar Schlemmer Theatre
Estate, IT - 28824 Oggebbio (VB), Italy

■ **Joost Schmidt** (1893-1948)
Germany

91 / p.9
**State Bauhaus Exhibition /
Weimar** 1923
Poster: lithograph
68.6 × 48.2 cm
© DACS 2004

92 / Not illustrated
The New Chess Game 1923
Design for poster: ink, pencil
40 × 41.1 cm

■ **Paul Schuitema** (1897-1973)
The Netherlands

93 / p.28
**Every Berkel is a Proved
Machine** 1926
Weighing machines
advertisement: letterpress
21 × 29.2 cm

94 / p.28
Nutricia Milk Powder c.1926
Advertisement: letterpress
36.8 × 30 cm

95 / p.28
Toledo Berkel 85000
1926
Weighing machine
advertisement: letterpress
29.8 × 22.2 cm

96 / p.27
**Central Union of 30,000
Transport Workers** 1930
Poster: lithograph
115.5 × 75.2 cm

■ **Kurt Schwitters** (1887-1948)
Germany

97 / Not illustrated
Amsterdam 1923
Collage: cut papers, printed
letters, rubber stamp
21 × 14.6 cm

98 / p.77
Merz = Kurt Schwitters 1923
Poster: lithograph
46.2 × 58.5 cm
© DACS 2004

99 / p.76
**Dammerstock / Exhibition of
Housing / Karlsruhe** 1929
Poster: lithograph
83 × 58 cm
© DACS 2004

100 / p.77
New Typographic Design
1930
Booklet: letterpress
14.9 × 21.2 cm (open)
© DACS 2004

■ **Kurt Schwitters**
and **Theo van Doesburg**
The Netherlands

101 / p.22
Little Dada Soirée 1923
Poster: lithograph
30.2 x 29.9 cm

■ **Nikolai Sidelnikov**
(1905-1994)
USSR

102 / p.56
Advertising Technique, No.2
1930
Design for magazine cover:
gelatin silver print, gouache
32.1 × 25.7 cm

103 / p.56
Bicycle Sport c.1930
Design for book cover:
collage, gouache, ink,
pencil
30.2 × 23.5 cm

104 / p.56
**The Time, the Energy,
the Will** c.1930
Photomontage: gouache,
photogravure, ink, pencil,
cut paper
33.2 × 25.1 cm

105 / Not illustrated
The Woman Worker c.1930
Design for book cover:
collage, gouache, ink, pencil
32.1 × 25.7 cm

106 / Not illustrated
Untitled 1930
Photogram: gelatin silver
print
23.8 × 17.5 cm

107 / Not illustrated
Untitled (#48) c.1930
Photomontage: gouache,
pencil, ink, photogravure,
cut paper
25.4 × 17.8 cm

108 / p.57
Untitled (#71) c.1930
Photomontage: gouache,
photogravure, ink, pencil,
lithograph
36.2 × 25.6 cm

109 / p.56
Untitled (#92) c.1930
Photomontage: gouache,
ink, photogravure,
lithograph
26.8 × 20.5 cm

■ **Mart Stam** (1899-1986)
The Netherlands

110 / p.23
**International Architecture
Exhibition / Rotterdam** 1928
Poster: letterpress
100.6 × 66.2 cm

■ **Vladimir Stenberg**
(1899-1982)
and **Georgii Stenberg**
(1900-1933)
USSR

111 / p.55
**High Society Wager /
Director Carl Froelich** 1927
Film poster: lithograph
107.5 × 71.2 cm
© DACS 2004

112 / p.53
**Symphony of a Great City /
Director Walter Ruttmann**
1928
Film poster: lithograph
107.9 × 70.5 cm
© DACS 2004

113 / p.55
The Eleventh Year / Director
Dziga Vertov 1928
Film poster: lithograph
103.5 × 70.5 cm
© DACS 2004

■ **Varvara Stepanova**
(1894-1958)
USSR

114 / p.47
**Tarelkin's Death /
Meyerhold Theatre** 1922
Poster: letterpress
68.6 × 104.8 cm
© DACS 2004

115 / Not illustrated
**Vladimir Mayakovsky /
Menacing Laughter** 1932
Book endpapers: lithograph
24.5 × 43.4 cm

■ **Varvara Stepanova**
and **Boris Ignatovitch**
(1899-1976)
USSR

116 / p.44
**Strengthen the Defence with
Whatever You Can** c.1934
Design for book cover: gelatin
silver print, red paper
24 × 17.4 cm
© DACS 2004

■ **Wladyslaw Strzemiński**
(1893-1952)
Poland

117 / p.81
From Beyond 1930
Book: letterpress
21.6 × 19.1 cm

■ **Ladislav Sutnar** (1897-1976)
Czechoslovakia

118 / p.84
**Exhibition of Modern
Trade / Brno** 1929
Poster: lithograph
46.8 × 62.7 cm
© Ladislav Sutnar. Permission of the
Ladislav Sutnar Family / Photo: Mike Fear

119 / p.85
**Exhibition of the
Harmonious Home** 1930
Poster: lithograph
95.3 × 60.8 cm
© Ladislav Sutnar. Permission of the
Ladislav Sutnar Family

120 / p.84
**International Exhibition of
Toys and Educational
Materials** c.1930
Poster: letterpress
46.7 × 62.8 cm
© Ladislav Sutnar. Permission of the
Ladislav Sutnar Family / Photo: Mike Fear

121 / p.83
Motorist and the Law 1932
Book cover: letterpress,
lithograph
22 × 16.6 cm
© Ladislav Sutnar. Permission of
the Ladislav Sutnar Family

122 / Not illustrated
**Prague State School of
Graphic Arts** 1932
Prospectus: letterpress
21 × 15 cm

123 / p.83
The Minimal House 1933
Proof of book cover:
letterpress
21 × 15 cm
© Ladislav Sutnar. Permission of
the Ladislav Sutnar Family

■ **Mieczyslaw Szczuka**
(1898-1927)
and **Teresa Zarnower**
(1895-1950)
Poland

124 / p.10
Europa
(Poem by Anatol Stern) 1929
Booklet: letterpress,
lithograph
29.6 × 27.6 cm
Photo: Mike Fear

■ **Karel Teige** (1900-1951)
Czechoslovakia

125 / p.82
Fragment (a) 1928
Reworked page from K. Biebl,
*With a Ship Importing Tea
and Coffee*: lithograph,
watercolour
19 × 13.7 cm
© Karel Teige heirs

126 / p.82
Fragment (b) 1928
Reworked page from K. Biebl,
*With a Ship Importing Tea
and Coffee*: lithograph,
watercolour
19 × 13.7 cm
© Karel Teige heirs

127 / p.82
**International Exhibition of
New Architecture** 1929
Poster: lithograph
64 × 95.3 cm
© Karel Teige heirs

■ **Solomon Telingater**
(1903-1969)
USSR

128 / p.61
**Ten Posters of Exercise
and Sports 1**
1928/29
Design for poster: gelatin
silver prints, photogravure,
gouache, coloured paper
31.1 × 25.1 cm
© DACS 2004

129 / p.61
**Ten Posters of Exercise
and Sports 2**
1928/29
Design for poster: gelatin
silver prints, photogravure,
gouache, coloured paper
31.8 × 26.2 cm
© DACS 2004

130 / p.61
**Ten Posters of Exercise
and Sports 3**
1928/29
Design for poster: gelatin
silver prints, photogravure,
gouache, coloured paper
31.8 × 26.7 cm
© DACS 2004

131 / p.61
**Ten Posters of Exercise
and Sports 4**
1928/29
Design for poster: gelatin
silver prints, photogravure,
gouache, coloured paper
31.1 × 25.1 cm
© DACS 2004

132 / p.60
Theatre of the Red Army
1928/29
Design for poster: gelatin
silver prints, photogravure,
gouache, coloured paper,
hand lettering
30 × 38.7 cm
© DACS 2004

133 / p.59
Stretching *c.*1929
Collage: ink, watercolour,
crayon, decorative paper,
gelatin silver prints, printed
letters, illustrations
34.9 × 22.9 cm
© DACS 2004

134 / p.58
Kirsanov has the Floor 1930
Booklet: letterpress
20.3 × 9.2 cm
© DACS 2004 / Photo: Mike Fear

■ **Georg Trump** (1896-1985)
Germany

135 / p.21
**Exhibition / School of
Applied Arts / Bielefeld** 1927
Design for poster: gelatin
silver print, printed letters,
pencil
58.5 × 45.7 cm

136 / p.67
The Photographic Image
1930
Poster: lithograph with
pasted-in paper correction
59.8 × 81.3 cm

■ **Jan Tschichold** (1902-1974)
Germany / Switzerland

137 / p.79
***The Trousers* / Director Hans
Behrendt** 1927
Film poster: lithograph
119.6 × 84.1 cm

138 / p.78
***The Woman Without a
Name*, Part Two / Director
Georg Jacoby** 1928
Film poster: lithograph
123.8 × 86.3 cm

139 / p.89
**Constructivists / Kunsthalle
Basel** 1937
Exhibition poster: lithograph
90.5 × 63.5 cm

■ **Hendrik Nicolaas
Werkman** (1882-1945)
The Netherlands

140 / p.30
***The Next Call*, No.7**
1926
Magazine: letterpress
42.6 × 54.6 cm (open)
Reproduced with permission by the
H.N. Werkman Foundation,
Amsterdam / Groningen

141 / p.30
***The Next Call*, No. 8**
1926
Magazine: letterpress
21.6 × 27.6 cm
Reproduced with permission by the
H.N. Werkman Foundation,
Amsterdam / Groningen

■ **Hendrikus Wijdeveld**
(1885-1989)
The Netherlands

142 / p.25
**International Economic-
Historical Exhibition /
Amsterdam** 1929
Poster: lithograph
64.8 × 50 cm

143 / p.24
**Architecture Exhibition /
Frank Lloyd Wright** 1931
Poster: letterpress
77.5 × 76.8 cm

■ **Piet Zwart** (1885-1977)
The Netherlands

144 / p.31
Verloop Estate Agents 1923
Poster: lithograph
44.5 × 44.5 cm
© DACS 2004

145 / p.32
Homage to a Young Woman
1925
Typographic experiment:
letterpress
24.2 × 17 cm
© DACS 2004

146 / p.32
NKF Paper Insulation 1925
Advertisement: letterpress
29.7 × 21.1 cm
© DACS 2004

147 / p.32
N.C.W. Cable 1926
Catalogue: letterpress
30 × 32 cm
© DACS 2004

148 / p.33
**International Exhibition of
Film / The Hague** 1928
Poster: lithograph
108 × 77.8 cm
© DACS 2004

149 / p.32
Trio Printers 1931
Page from booklet:
letterpress
29.5 × 20.8 cm
© DACS 2004

Selected Bibliography

Ades, Dawn, *Photomontage*, Thames and Hudson, London,1986.

Ades, Dawn, *The Twentieth Century Poster: Design of the Avant-Garde*, Abbeville Press, New York,1994.

Aynsley, Jeremy, *Graphic Design in Germany 1890-1945*, Thames & Hudson, London, 2000.

Bonnel, Victoria E, *Iconography of Power: Soviet Political Posters under Lenin and Stalin*, University of California Press, Berkeley and Los Angeles,1997.

Broos, Kees, and Hefting, Paul, *Dutch Graphic Design*, Phaidon, London,1993.

Compton, Susan, *Russian Avant-Garde Books 1917-1934*, The British Library, London,1992.

Dickerman, Leah (ed.), *Building the Collective: Soviet Graphic Design 1917-1937: Selections from the Merrill C. Berman Collection*, Princeton Architectural Press, New York,1996.

Fernandez, Horacio, *Fotografia Publica: Photography in Print 1919-1939*, Aldeasa, Madrid,1999.

Hollis, Richard, *Graphic Design: A Concise History*, Thames and Hudson, London,1994.

Kinross, Robin, *Modern Typography: An essay in critical history*, Hyphen Press, London,1992.

Lodder, Christina, *Russian Constructivism*, Yale University Press, New Haven and London,1983.

Margolin, Victor, *The Struggle for Utopia: Rodchenko, Lissitzky, Moholy-Nagy*, University of Chicago Press,Chicago,1997.

Overy, Paul, *De Stijl*, Thames and Hudson, London,1991.

Rothschild, Deborah, Lupton, Ellen and Goldstein, Darra, *Graphic Design in the Mechanical Age: Selections from the Merrill C. Berman Collection*, Yale University Press, New Haven and London,1983.

Spencer, Herbert (ed), *The Liberated Page*, Lund Humphries, London,1987,1990.

Spencer, Herbert, *Pioneers of Modern Typography*, Lund Humphries, London,1982.

Rowell, Margit, and Wye, Deborah, *The Russian Avant-Garde Book 1910-1934*, The Museum of Modern Art, New York, 2002.